· 16406

D0342890

# THE

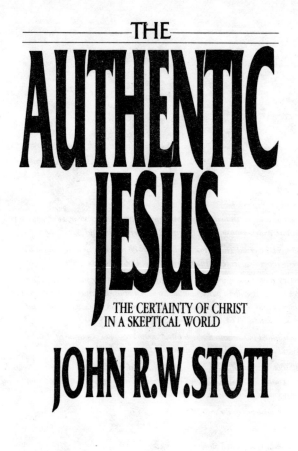

# AUTHENTIC JESUS

### THE CERTAINTY OF CHRIST
### IN A SKEPTICAL WORLD

# JOHN R.W. STOTT

INTERVARSITY PRESS
DOWNERS GROVE, ILLINOIS 60515

*InterVarsity Press is the book-publishing division of Inter-Varsity Christian Fellowship, a student movement active on campus at hundreds of universities, colleges and schools of nursing. For information about local and regional activities, write IVCF, 233 Langdon St., Madison, WI 53703.*

*Distributed in Canada through InterVarsity Press, 860 Denison St., Unit 3, Markham, Ontario L3R 4H1, Canada.*

*All Bible quotations unless otherwise indicated, are from the Holy Bible, New International Version. Copyright © 1973, 1978, International Bible Society. Used by permission of Zondervan Bible Publishers.*

*Cover illustration: Roberta Polfus*

*ISBN 0-87784-619-7*

*Printed in the United States of America*

---

**Library of Congress Cataloging in Publication Data**

*Stott, John R. W.*
  *The authentic Jesus.*

  *Bibliography: p.*
  *1. Jesus Christ—Person and offices.  I. Title.*
*BT202.S749        1985        232        85-23831*
*ISBN 0-87784-619-7*

---

| 14 | 13 | 12 | 11 | 10 | 9 | 8 | 7 | 6 | 5 | 4 | 3 | 2 | 1 |
|----|----|----|----|----|---|---|---|---|---|---|---|---|---|
| 96 | 95 | 94 | 93 | 92 | 91 | 90 | 89 | 88 | 87 | 86 | 85 | | |

# Preface

This short book is a tract for the times. It attempts to respond to certain theological statements and publications which during the last seven or eight years have disturbed Christian people in Britain. In particular, I refer to *The Myth of God Incarnate* (1977), some recent well-publicized utterances of Dr. David Jenkins, Bishop of Durham, and an Anglican report entitled *Towards a Theology for Inter-Faith Dialogue* (1984). These all in their different ways either question or deny traditional understandings of Jesus Christ.

The reason I have referred to and quoted from particular documents is that I have felt it important to ground the discussion in reality and to relate my response to actual statements. The debate is about principles not personalities, however.

Moreover, the views I am challenging are much more widely held than by the individuals I have named. Since they are current in the United States, I am glad that this American edition is being published.

John Stott
July 1985

# 1
# INTRODUCTION: THE PRESENT CONTROVERSY

$W$e preach Christ crucified" (1 Cor 1:23). "We preach
. . . Jesus Christ as Lord" (2 Cor 4:5 RSV). With these two
affirmations Paul summed up the heart of the apostles'
message. It centered on the historical person of Jesus of
Nazareth who first died a shameful death by crucifixion
(on account of which, however, our sins may be forgiven)
and was then exalted by God as the supreme Lord over
all.

The church has continued to proclaim the same good
news. It is true that the Christian faith is a Trinitarian faith.
We believe in God as Creator, Sustainer and Father. We
also believe in the Holy Spirit as the Spirit of truth who
spoke through the prophets and apostles and who sanc-
tifies the people of God. But, above all, our testimony is

directed to Jesus Christ, Son of the Father and giver of the Spirit, who was conceived and born, suffered and was crucified, died, was buried and went to the dead, rose again, ascended, reigns and will come back to judge. The disproportion of clauses in the Apostles' Creed clearly exhibits the Christ-centered nature of the Christian faith; it contains only three relating to the Father and five relating to the work of the Spirit but thirteen which speak of the Son.

## Under Attack

It is for this reason, and understandably so, that Christians feel very defensive when the church's traditional faith in Jesus is under attack.

Yet this has been the situation during at least the past decade or so. In 1977 the symposium entitled *The Myth of God Incarnate* was published. Its contributors were seven academic theologians from Cambridge, Oxford and Birmingham Universities, and its editor was John Hick. It was a confusing book, as many symposia are, since its authors evidently held different positions. It also bore an irresponsible title, since the word *myth* was used in the text in several different senses, ranging from "mystery" (which all Christians affirm about the incarnation) to "a fiction with symbolic meaning but no historical foundation" (which no Christian can affirm about the incarnation and remain recognizably a Christian). Certainly the overall thrust of the book was to deny the traditional Christian conviction that Jesus of Nazareth was both God and man.

"Buddhology and Christology," wrote John Hick, "developed in comparable ways." That is, both grew out of the religious devotion of their followers, until each "came to be thought of" as an incarnation. It was a gradual process of "deification." [1] (He fails to add that divine honors were not accorded to the Buddha until long after his death, whereas Jesus was already being worshiped immediately after his death and resurrection, if not actually during his lifetime.) "It is natural," John Hick has written elsewhere, "that those who found through Jesus a decisive encounter with God, and a new and better life, hailed him as 'Son of God', and that later this poetry should have hardened into prose, and escalated from a metaphorical Son of God to a metaphysical God the Son."[2]

Who was Jesus, then, in the opinion of these theologians? The question was put to John Hick at the press conference which launched the *Myth* book. "He was a wonderful man," Professor Hick replied, provoking laughter in the unbelieving reporters who were present, "perhaps the most wonderful man who has ever lived, intensely open to God."

Since then one of the contributors to the symposium, Michael Goulder, concluding that he no longer believed in God, had the honor and courage to resign his position as an ordained Christian minister. But Don Cupitt, another contributor, although he now describes himself as a "Christian Buddhist" and has been candid about his unbelief in *Taking Leave of God* (1980), continues as dean of Emmanuel College, Cambridge, and somehow contrives in the pursuit of his duties in chapel to say or sing "Glory be to the Father, and to the Son, and to the Holy Spirit."

The year 1984, which George Orwell predicted would witness the totalitarian suppression of all deviant opinions, turned out on the contrary to be a year in which (at least in the church) they have been freely and even flagrantly expressed. It was in this year that the hitherto little-known David Jenkins, professor of theology at the University of Leeds, became bishop designate of Durham. At that time he had the reputation of being fairly conservative in his faith. For in his 1966 Bampton Lectures, entitled *The Glory of Man,* he committed himself to the Chalcedonian Definition (A.D. 451) of the person of Jesus Christ. "God and man are distinct realities," he wrote, "who, in and as Jesus Christ, are in perfect union."[3] Then in 1974 he gave the Edward Cadbury Lectures at Birmingham University which were published two years later under the title *The Contradiction of Christianity.* The book was an exploration into what it means to be human, and in the final chapter David Jenkins committed himself to the doctrine of the Trinity. "The symbol of the Trinity," he wrote, "insists on and lays claim to a unique way of holding together transcendence and immanence, eternity and history, God and human beings." Indeed, it is "the necessary and legitimate interpretation of the experienced and perceived story of God, Jesus and the Spirit."[4]

David Jenkins's friends were not surprised, therefore, when he was appointed a bishop, nor when he described himself as a "believing" not a "doubting" bishop, nor when he said that he responded to the questions put to him at his consecration "unhesitatingly," "affirmatively" and "in complete good faith." Yet both before and after his consecration he has expressed doubts about, and has seemed actually to deny, the historicity of both the virgin birth and the bodily resurrection of Jesus. The media publicized his views (with varying degrees of accuracy) throughout the world. Agnostics were confirmed in their skepticism, since they shared the bishop's position. But the faith of the faithful was disturbed. So it is important for us to be clear about the issue. Bishop Jenkins says he affirms the incarnation and the resurrection, but questions the virgin birth and the empty tomb. Is his position tenable?

Let us begin by setting this current debate within the broad context of history. The church has hardly ever enjoyed a period of unruffled doctrinal calm. Theological controversy is by no means a twentieth-century novelty. On the contrary, there have always been professedly Christian teachers who have questioned, criticized and challenged received orthodoxy. The experience is painful for all concerned. At the same time, it turns out to be creative if believers emerge from it with their understanding refined, their faith strengthened and their minds better equipped to engage the dilemmas of the contemporary world. My first concern, then, is to urge my fellow Christians, if I may borrow some of Paul's words about a controversy of his own day, "not to become easily unsettled or alarmed" (2 Thess 2:2), however exalted the source of the attack, but rather to grapple with the issues involved.

## The Presuppositions of Unbelief
The roots of the 1984 debate can be traced back to the Enlightenment, which at the beginning of the eighteenth century attempted to replace revelation by reason, dogma

by inquiry, God by nature, and priest by scientist. As Bishop Lesslie Newbigin has written in his book *The Other Side of 1984,* the churches at that time feebly "surrendered the public sphere to control by the assumptions of the Enlightenment, and survived by retreating into the private sector." We are still suffering from the church's loss of nerve. It is time, Bishop Newbigin continues, for Christians to go over to the offensive and to mount "a genuinely missionary encounter with post-Enlightenment culture."[5] This will call for great intellectual clarity and courage.

In particular, the parties to the debate will need to examine their presuppositions. Those who deny the possibility of miracles in the physical order—whether the virgin birth or bodily resurrection or nature miracles which are attributed to Jesus in the Gospels—do so in the name of the scientific revolution. Science has shown the universe to be a closed system, they say, in which there is an inflexible uniformity of cause and effect, and therefore miracles are *a priori* excluded. Moreover, those who still believe in them, they continue, are trying to retain a prescientific world view that is totally outmoded and can only be defended as "mythological."

What these thinkers often fail to perceive, however, is that they too have their presuppositions, which in their case are those of scientific secularism. How can they deny the very possibility of miracles and at the same time confess their faith in God? What kind of God do they believe in? Do they really imagine that they can lock the living God the Creator within his universe, permitting him no deviations from the so-called laws of nature and no intrusions into his own creation? It is significant that during the controversy over Bishop Jenkins's denial of miracles, a group of fourteen scientists, most of whom were university professors in different disciplines, and whose spokesman was the geneticist Professor R. J. Berry, president of the Linnean Society, wrote a letter to *The Times* ( 13 July 1984), which included the following comments:

It is not logically valid to use science as an argument against miracles. To believe that miracles cannot happen is as much an act of faith as to believe that they can happen.

We gladly accept the virgin birth, the Gospel miracles, and the resurrection of Christ as historical events. We know that we are representative of many other scientists who are also Christians standing in the historical tradition of the churches.

Miracles are unprecedented events. Whatever the current fashions in philosophy or the revelations of opinion polls may suggest, it is important to affirm that science (based as it is upon the observation of precedents) can have nothing to say on the subject. Its "laws" are only generalisations of our experience. Faith rests on other grounds.

**True and Reasonable**

Our quarrel, then, is not with the questions which are being asked, but with the answers which are being given and with the secular presuppositions which lie behind them. Critical scrutiny of the credentials of Christianity is indispensable. Sensitivity to the real questions of the modern world is, moreover, essential to Christian maturity.

And evangelism is impossible without it. We shall not win people to Christ by ignoring their problems. The apostles were constantly "arguing" with people out of the Scriptures. Paul's confident claim before Festus was that what he was saying was "true and reasonable" (Acts 26:25). It does not seem to have occurred to him that apologetics and evangelism were incompatible, or that reasoning was inconsistent with trust in the Holy Spirit. On the contrary, he could describe all his evangelistic activity and purpose with the words "we persuade men" (2 Cor 5:11 RSV).

Questions are one thing, however, together with the need to face them with integrity; denials are another. Church leaders have a right, even a duty, to ask penetrating questions which induce both believers and unbelievers to think. But it is extremely serious if they deny (or even appear to deny) fundamentals of the traditional Christian faith which they have solemnly undertaken to guard, expound and proclaim.

What, then, is the proper response to the searching questions of our day? There are three possible options. The first is to capitulate too quickly to the contemporary mood and to revise the faith in light of it. The motive behind this accommodation is often admirable, namely, the anxiety to make the gospel intelligible to modern men and women. But those who take this road tend to forget Dean W. R. Inge's aphorism that "he who marries the spirit of this age will find himself a widower in the next." The second option is to be avoided too, however. This is to ignore the contemporary obstacles to faith and simply reassert traditional belief with unself-critical dogmatism. The third and wisest way is to listen attentively to the problems being raised and the questions being asked, and then restate the gospel in such a way as to take account of them.

This is the way which I am to attempt in this book. I am writing with thoughtful Christians in mind, who have had little or no formal theological education, but are nevertheless determined to have themselves, and be able to give to others, sound reasons for the Christian hope they cherish (1 Pet 3:15). Another characteristic of the readers I envisage is their humility. One of the most distressing features of some recent statements by church leaders is the patronizing, even arrogant, way in which they have dismissed opposing views as being held only by the "unsophisticated." The essential condition of receiving light from heaven is not sophistication, however, but simplicity. For the Lord of the universe has "hidden these things from the wise and learned," Jesus said, "and revealed them to little children" (Mt 11:25).

Who, then, is the authentic Jesus?

# 2
# THE FIRST
# WITNESSES

$O$ur knowledge of Jesus of Nazareth comes almost entirely from the New Testament. The few references to him in Roman literature (especially by Tacitus, Suetonius and Pliny) and in Jewish literature (by Josephus) are all brief, not equally reliable, and, although they are valuable for their independent confirmation of Jesus' life, death and following, they really add nothing to what we learn from the Gospels. So we are largely limited to these Christian documents. But can we trust them? This is a huge question, especially after a century of meticulous Gospel "criticism" by which scholars have investigated the text itself, its literary sources, cultural backgrounds, historical origins in the life of the primitive Christian communities, and the forms in which they preserved and taught the words and works of Jesus. All I can hope to do in the brief compass of these pages is to give reasons why I believe the customary skepticism about the Gospels is inappropriate and why we should approach them with confidence rather than suspicion.

## Witnesses

First, the Gospel writers had a serious purpose, namely, to be *witnesses*. Indeed, the primary purpose of the whole Bible is to bear witness to Jesus Christ. God has given us in Scripture his own testimony to his Son, although he gave it through human witnesses. The Old Testament Scriptures, Jesus said, testify to him (Jn 5:39). The New Testament Scriptures have the same purpose, for they contain the record and interpretation of Jesus given by the apostolic eyewitnesses and those associated with them in the earliest believing communities. What John wrote about his Gospel is applicable to the rest of the New Testament. The words and signs of Jesus which he recorded were "written that you may believe that Jesus is the Christ, the Son of God, and that by believing you may have life in his name" (Jn 20:31; see also 2 Tim 3:15).

The Gospel writers are therefore correctly called "evangelists," and their literary compositions are rightly called "gospels" (which means "good news"). For it was not their intention to write a comprehensive history or biography of Jesus in the modern sense of those terms. Instead, they were setting forth the good news of Jesus Christ, with a view to inducing their readers to believe in him. In consequence, they deliberately selected, arranged and shaped their material in such a way as to serve their evangelistic purpose. Each Gospel writer had a discernible theological purpose. To oversimplify, Matthew presents Jesus as the fulfillment of Old Testament prophecy; Mark, as the suffering servant of the Lord; Luke, as the universal Savior of sinners; and John, as the eternal Logos or Son of God. The great merit of so-called redaction criticism (*redaction* means "editing") is that it attributes the contents and emphasis of each Gospel not so much to the needs of the local community within which it may have taken shape, as it does to the particular doctrinal purpose of the "redactor" (editor) or "evangelist."

## Historians

Second, the Gospel writers were not only witnesses, evangelists and theologians; they were *historians* as well. We would naturally expect this, because the living God of the whole biblical revelation is the God of history, whose purposes are being fulfilled in a historical process which had a beginning and, with equal certainty, will have an end. The people of God had a beginning, when God called Abraham. The universe, the planet Earth and human beings all had a beginning too. So the God of the Bible is the God of creation and of the covenant; the God of Abraham, Isaac and Jacob; the God of Moses and of the exodus from Egypt; the God of the judges and the kings, the prophets and the wise men. Above all, he is the God and Father of our Lord Jesus Christ, whose most mighty act was performed through the birth, life, death, resurrection and exaltation of Christ, culminating in the gift of his Spirit and the birth of his church.

To these mighty acts of God in history the prophets and

apostles bore witness. They recorded them as historical events and went on to unfold their saving significance. We must never set theology and history over against each other, since Scripture refuses to do so. The history it records is "salvation history," and the salvation it proclaims was achieved by means of historical events.

None of the other evangelists outlines his purpose more fully than Luke in the preface to his Gospel. Here is what he writes:

Many have undertaken to draw up an account of the things that have been fulfilled among us, just as they were handed down to us by those who from the first were eyewitnesses and servants of the word. Therefore, since I myself have carefully investigated everything from the beginning, it seemed good also to me to write an orderly account for you, most excellent Theophilus, so that you may know the certainty of the things you have been taught. (1:1-4)

It is most instructive to trace the four stages which Luke outlines.

First, certain "things" had "been fulfilled among us." This without doubt is an allusion to the events of the earthly career of Jesus. Not only had they happened, historically speaking, but Luke's chosen verb ("fulfilled") may also indicate that their occurrence, far from being fortuitous, was in deliberate fulfillment of God's Old Testament promises.

Second, these things were seen by "eyewitnesses," who went on to testify to what they had seen and heard. Moreover, their witness was not restricted to their contemporaries. For they "handed down" these things (as a tradition) to the next generation, who had not themselves been eyewitnesses. This second generation included Luke, who here acknowledges his dependence on the first-generation eyewitnesses.

Third, the tradition which emanated from the original eyewitnesses did not remain oral. No, "many" had undertaken to "draw up an account" of what had happened. So Luke followed suit. He clearly states his qualification, namely, that he had "carefully investigated everything from the beginning." That is, he had not taken everything on trust from the apostolic eyewitnesses; he had personally checked what had been handed down to him. When and how he did this we do not know, but we can make a guess. He tells us (by one of his unobtrusive "we" sections in Acts) that he arrived in Palestine with Paul after the third missionary journey (21:15), and that about two and a half years later he left with Paul on their journey to Rome (27:1). During most of the interim period Paul was in prison in Caesarea (24:27). But Luke was a free man. He does not tell us how he occupied his time, but the strong probability is that he traveled the length and breadth of the Holy Land, visiting the sacred sites associated with the ministry of Jesus and interviewing the people who had known and heard him.

Fourth, Luke discloses the purpose he had in mind when writing down and publishing the results of his investigations. It was for the benefit of one Theophilus, evidently a high-ranking Roman official ("most excellent"), perhaps his patron, apparently a new convert, who had been "taught" about Jesus. Luke wanted him (and doubtless others like him) to "know the certainty" of what he had been taught.

Here, then, are the four stages Luke delineates. First, the events. Then the eyewitness tradition. Next the written accounts, including Luke's. And finally the certainty which these brought to their readers. Now this is not the language of one who is writing unhistorical myths. No, his claim is entirely different and absolutely clear. He has personally and carefully investigated what the eyewitnesses had passed on. He has written an orderly account of what their traditions and his investigations have revealed. And he believes that his writing is reliable enough to lead Theophilus and others to certainty about Jesus. It seems to me that modern scholars have no warrant at all for setting aside Luke's painstakingly worded claim.

**Christians**

In the third place, the Gospel writers, who were theologians and evangelists on the one hand and historians on the other, were also credible witnesses because they were *Christians*. Is this too obvious and simple a point to make? I think not, for it is often overlooked. Most of us, before we buy or read a book, want to know something about its author, about his or her character and qualifications for writing. Is the author trustworthy? It is the same with the Gospels. Mark and Luke were almost certainly the writers of the second and third Gospels, but there is continuing debate about how the names of Matthew and John came to be attached to the first and fourth. Nevertheless, whatever uncertainty there may be about the identity of the four Gospel writers, there is no uncertainty about the fact that they were all dedicated followers of the

Lord Jesus. And the Lord Jesus they followed (according to one of them) said he had come to bear witness to the truth, claimed even to be himself the truth, and added that the truth would set them free (Jn 8:32; 14:6; 18:37). The other three, who did not record those sayings, nevertheless portrayed Jesus as one who taught with authority and conviction, and who abominated hypocrisy more than anything else. We can assert without fear of contradiction, therefore, that the evangelists were themselves honest men. They were not deceivers. They were witnesses, and they knew the stringent Old Testament requirements that witnesses must be true, not false.

Their honesty is confirmed as we read the Gospels. For they contain internal evidence of their authors' impartiality. For one thing, they include mysterious sayings of Jesus which, for fear of misinterpretation, they might have preferred to omit, like the question of why the rich young ruler called Jesus "good" when only God was good, Jesus' shrinking from death in the garden of Gethsemane and his cry of God-forsakenness on the cross. The evangelists also include incidents about themselves which now, as leaders of the church, they would doubtless rather forget, like their misunderstandings of Jesus, the selfish request of James and John for the most honorable seats in the kingdom and Peter's shameful threefold denial of his Lord. But they make no attempt to hush up their earlier failings. These evidences of their integrity further establish our confidence in them as authors.

**Believers in God**
Fourth, in addition to being theologians, historians and

followers of Jesus, the Gospel writers were *believers in God.* Never mind exactly how they would have articulated it, they believed that God had said and done something unique through Jesus. With Jesus the long-awaited new eon had dawned. Through Jesus, God's long-promised reign of righteousness and peace had broken into history. The time had been fulfilled, and the kingdom of God had begun.

This sense of newness pervades their writings. Jesus had established the new covenant by his blood. Those who are in him experience a new creation. They are a new community. They have already tasted the powers of the new age. We believe this too. One could hardly claim to be a Christian and not believe that the Christ-event is epoch-making and marks the watershed of human history. My point in emphasizing it is this: can we believe that God said and did something through Jesus, which was decisive for the salvation of humankind, and that he then allowed this word and deed to be lost in the mists of antiquity? Such a contradiction is impossible. Instead, it is reasonable in itself, and congruous with the Old Testament pattern, to affirm that the God who spoke and acted uniquely through Jesus would also make provision for his revelation and redemption to be written down by reliable witnesses so that future generations throughout the world might partake of their benefits too.

The church has an apologetic task in every age to defend and demonstrate the reliability of its foundational documents. For then we can go further and challenge our own contemporaries to read the New Testament for themselves and not rely on secondhand accounts of it, let alone dismiss what they have never personally investigated. It is more important to persuade people to expose themselves to the testimony of the original apostolic eyewitnesses than it is to get them to listen to our own testimony. Our testimony can indeed corroborate theirs, as experience confirms history. But it is "through their message," Jesus said, that people would come to believe (Jn 17:20), as the Holy Spirit himself, who is always the chief witness, carries it home to the mind, heart and conscience of the readers.

## For Further Reading

F. F. Bruce, *The New Testament Documents: Are They Reliable?* (IVP, 1960).

John R. W. Stott, *God's Book for God's People* (IVP, 1982).

# 3
# JESUS: MAN AND GOD

*T*he traditional Christian belief, revealed in the New Testament and formulated by the early church, is that Jesus of Nazareth, although one person, was and is both God and man. Yet this foundational Christian doctrine is being increasingly criticized and even denied, for example in *The Myth of God Incarnate,* as we saw earlier. Can we continue with intellectual integrity to believe it?

## The God-Man
We should begin by affirming that Jesus was a real and complete human being. He so identified with the human race as to become truly one of us. Everything which is indispensable to authentic humanness can confidently be predicated of Jesus. He was born like us. He developed

from infancy through childhood and youth to adult life just as we do. His body was subject to the same physiological conditions as ours is. He ate and drank, slept and sweated, became tired and felt pain, suffered, died, was buried and went to the dead, like other human beings. If his body was human, so were his emotions. He experienced love and anger, indignation and compassion, sorrow and joy. He was also tempted just as we are, even savagely by the devil's direct assaults, although he never succumbed to them and therefore never sinned.

During his earthly human life and ministry Jesus was dependent on his Father just as we are. He therefore needed to pray. He acknowledged both that he could do nothing without his Father's power and that he taught only what his Father had shown him. He thus ascribed all his words and works to his Father. It is doubtless because of his dependence on his Father's revelation that he could even make the astonishing statement that he did not know the day of his return (Mk 13:32). Only his Father knew it and evidently had not divulged it—hence his ignorance of it in spite of his supernatural knowledge in other fields. All this evidence supports the New Testament's description of him as "the man Christ Jesus" (1 Tim 2:5).

But the Christian conviction has always been that the man Christ Jesus is also God. Not a man with divine qualities, nor God appearing in human disguise, but God the eternal Son (or Word) who actually "became flesh" (Jn 1:14). The four great Ecumenical Councils of the fourth and fifth centuries all wrestled with the mysteries of the Christological question, and each pronounced on an aspect of it. The Council of Nicea (A.D. 325) affirmed that Jesus is truly God, and the Council of Constantinople (A.D. 381) that he is truly man. The Council of Ephesus (A.D. 431) added that, though God and man, he is one person, while the Council of Chalcedon (A.D. 451) clarified that, though one person, he is both God and man perfectly. The heart of the Chalcedonian Definition is as follows: "One and the selfsame Son, our Lord, is perfect in godhead, perfect in manhood, begotten of the Father eternally as to divinity, but born of the virgin temporally as to humanity. There is one Christ in two natures, unconfusedly, unchangeably, indivisibly and inseparably."

This beautifully succinct summary of Christian belief owed much to the clarity of Leo the Great, who became pope in A.D. 440. In his famous *Tome* he had written: "Christ is God and Christ is man. The two natures coexist. Neither nature diminishes anything or adds anything to the properties of the other." What Leo clarified and the Council of Chalcedon defined, the church has continued to teach. The sixteenth-century Reformers, for example, who did battle with the Church of Rome over the supremacy and sufficiency of Scripture and over justification by faith alone, saw no need to alter the Christological statements of the early centuries. Instead, they endorsed them. Thus, the second Anglican Article (1563) reads: "The Son, who is the Word of the Father, begotten from everlasting of the Father, the very and eternal God, and of one substance with the Father, took man's nature in the womb of the blessed virgin, of her substance, so that two whole and perfect natures, that is to say, the Godhead and the manhood, were joined together in one person, never to be divided, whereof is one Christ, very God and very man."

Moreover, the reason why the Reformers endorsed this teaching of the Council of Chalcedon is that they recognized its strong biblical basis. Leo in his *Tome* and the bishops in their council were neither speculating nor innovating. Their doctrine of the two natures of Christ was taught by the earliest fathers, for example, by Clement of Rome at the end of the first century, by Ignatius at the beginning of the second and by Tertullian at the beginning of the third, even if they differed somewhat on the unity of Christ's person.

More important still, it went right back to the New Testament. As B. B. Warfield wrote, "The Chalcedonian Christology . . . is only a very perfect synthesis of the biblical data,"[1] avoiding any overemphasis on either the deity of Jesus or his humanity or the oneness of his person. At Chalcedon "all the biblical data are brought together in a harmonious statement, in which each receives full recognition."[2] Indeed, the statement of the two natures in the one person is more than a New Testament synthesis; it is the foundation of the New Testament documents. "All teaching of the apostolic age rests on it as its universal presupposition."[3] And this presupposition is derived from Jesus' own self-consciousness and self-testimony, for he "ranked Himself above all creatures (Mk. xiii. 32)," lived on intimate terms with the Father, and yet "habitually spoke of Himself as 'the Son of Man.' "[4]

**Biblical Evidence**

What is the evidence, however, for the divine self-consciousness of Jesus? It is true that it is nowhere recorded in his teaching that he declared unambiguously "I am God." The nearest explicit statements are perhaps his "I and the Father are one" (Jn 10:30), which his hearers regarded as blasphemous, and Thomas's confession "my Lord and my God!" (Jn 20:28), which Jesus accepted. It was Thomas's unbelief which Jesus rebuked; he received and did not rebuke Thomas's worship.

More compelling than these isolated sayings are three claims of Jesus which he repeated so constantly that they are woven into the fabric of his teaching and cannot possibly be disentangled from it. The first was to be the fulfillment of the Old Testament Scriptures so that he was not so much another prophet as the fulfillment of all prophecy. His contemporaries' eyes and ears were actually seeing and hearing what had for centuries been foretold (Mt 13:16-17).

His second claim was to enjoy in his relationship with his Father an intimacy which was shared by nobody else (Mt 11:27) and which was expressed in the affectionate diminutive "Abba, Father."

Third, Jesus claimed to have authority over men and women to teach them about God, to call them to himself, to forgive their sins and to judge them on the last day. Although a human being himself, he thus set himself apart from and "over" other human beings.

We cannot escape these claims, which are the more impressive for being made unobtrusively and indirectly. He said he was the Christ of Scripture, the Son of God, and the Lord, Savior and Judge of humankind. Moreover, the sheer self-centeredness of his claims stands out in

stark contrast to the humility of his bearing and the un-
selfishness of his ministry. The One who said he was their
lord and judge became their servant and washed their
feet.

So the early Christians did not hesitate to call Jesus
"Lord" and themselves his "slaves." They did it in the full
knowledge that "the Lord" *(ho kurios)* was a divine title,
which those who had translated the Old Testament into
Greek had used for the Hebrew *Yahweh* and which the
Roman emperors also assumed when demanding that divine honors be accorded them. The early Christians not
only gave Jesus this Old Testament God-title; they went
on to transfer to Jesus Old Testament God-texts. For example, Yahweh had sworn that "every knee" would bow
to him and "every tongue" confess his name (Is 45:23);
but Paul, whether in an original utterance or in quoting
from an early Christian hymn, wrote that God had "super-
exalted" Jesus in order that every knee and every tongue
should pay homage to him (Phil 2:9-11). Again, the
prophet Joel had predicted that "everyone who calls on
the name of the LORD [Yahweh] will be saved" (2:32), but
the apostle Peter probably (Acts 2:21, 38) and the apostle
Paul definitely (for example, Rom 10:9-13) applied this
promise of salvation to those who call on the name of
Jesus.

This transfer of God-titles and God-texts from Yahweh
to Jesus has an unavoidable implication. It identifies Jesus
as God, who is able to save and who is worthy of worship.
That the early Christians acted on this conviction is incon-
trovertible. They looked to Jesus to save them, and they
humbled themselves before him in praise and prayer.

Before they were ready to formulate their faith in Jesus, they expressed it in their devotion to him. As Bishop Donald Coggan has put it, "It was a long time before the Creeds were to be hammered out or the great Church Councils held. But Christolatry preceded Christology prayer came before the definition of doctrine."[5]

This order is extremely important. The ultimate issue in relation to Jesus Christ is not one of semantics (the meaning of words) but of homage (the attitude of the heart), not whether our tongue can subscribe to an orthodox formulation of the person of Jesus but whether our knee has bowed before his majesty. Besides, reverence always precedes understanding. We shall know him only if we are willing to obey him (Jn 7:17).

I remember the occasion some years ago when four of the seven contributors to *The Myth of God Incarnate* came to London for a day's theological consultation (and confrontation) with a team of conservative theologians. During the lunch break I asked one of the *Myth* contributors the direct question "Do you ever worship Jesus?"

Instantly he replied, "No, never."

By this he identified himself out of his own mouth, for nobody can call himself a Christian who does not worship Jesus. To worship him, if he is not God, is idolatry; to withhold worship from him, if he is, is apostasy.

**For Further Reading**
Norman Anderson, *The Mystery of the Incarnation* (IVP, 1978).
Michael Green, ed., *The Truth of God Incarnate* (Eerdmans, 1977).
David F. Wells, *The Person of Christ* (Crossway, 1984).

# 4
# THE RESURRECTION OF JESUS CHRIST

*T*he death and resurrection of Jesus were at the very center of the apostles' message. Sometimes their emphasis seems to have been particularly on his resurrection, so that both the Jewish leaders in Jerusalem and the Greek philosophers in Athens understood their distinctive doctrine to be a linking of "Jesus" and "the resurrection" (Acts 4:2; 17:18). It would be a mistake, however, to deduce from this that they were proclaiming Jesus' resurrection at the expense of his death. It would be more accurate to say that his resurrection both presupposed his death and validated its efficacy, and that therefore they could not have preached either without the other. G. E. Ladd after a thorough survey of apostolic teaching could conclude: "The entire New Testament was written from the perspective of the resurrection. Indeed, the resurrection may be called the major premise of the early Christian faith."[1]

Yet the controversy surrounding Bishop Jenkins of Durham has focused on his apparent denial of the resurrection. True, he said to his diocesan synod in November 1984: "I do believe in the Resurrection of Jesus Christ our Lord from the dead. . . . Anyone who says that I do not believe in the Resurrection . . . is a liar. This I must say fiercely and categorically." He will not convince people merely by the use of fierce and intemperate language, however. The question is *in what sense* he believes in the resurrection. During the service in which he was consecrated a bishop he was asked: "Do you accept the doctrine of the Christian faith *as the Church of England has received it?*" He should have answered "no," for the Church of England has received the doctrine of the resurrection from the creeds, and ultimately from the Scriptures, and these clearly teach the empty tomb (as we shall see), which Bishop Jenkins questions and even denies.

In the BBC television program "Credo" in April 1984, which sparked the conflagration, David Jenkins was asked if he held the view that Jesus rose from the dead. He replied: "Well, I hold the view that he rose from the dead; the question is what that means, isn't it?" He went on to affirm that "the very life and power and purpose and personality which was in him [Jesus] was actually continuing . . . in the sphere of history, so that he was a risen and living presence and possibility." But this is not at all what the apostles or the creeds or the formularies of the Church of England mean by Jesus' resurrection. All Bishop Jenkins seems to believe is the rather vapid truism that the influence of Jesus lives on in the world. Is he saying any more about Jesus than the Latin American students are saying about Che Guevara when they chant "He lives," or than Greek Cypriot patriots were saying about Archbishop Makarios when after his death they spray-painted buildings with the words "Makarios lives"? The apostles meant much more than this. Does Bishop Jenkins? He owes it to the church to answer this crucial question.

Mind you, David Jenkins is not the only offender in this matter. Some very orthodox evangelicals are also to blame when they sing the popular chorus:

He lives! He lives!
Christ Jesus lives today.
He walks with me,
He talks with me,
Along life's narrow way.
He lives! He lives!
Salvation to impart.
You ask me how I know he lives?
He lives within my heart.

I guess that Bishop Jenkins could sing those words with gusto, for he affirms that Jesus "lives" and "saves," and the "heart" is as good a place as any in which to locate him. But to affirm the living presence of Jesus by his Spirit in our hearts is not the same as to affirm his resurrection. His indwelling presence is a continuing experience; his resurrection was a historical event. By it his body was transformed, his tomb became empty and the power of death was defeated.

There are two questions to ask about the resurrection.

First, did it happen? Second, does it matter whether it happened or not?

## Did It Happen?

Did it happen? Was Jesus "raised from death" in such a way that his body was changed and his tomb emptied? What is the truth about his resurrection? I was very sorry to read in a recent article by David Jenkins that, according to the letters he had received, there was "disturbing evidence of an absence of a concern for truth among the self-styled defenders of Christian faith and orthodoxy," and that there had been "hardly any discussion of the case for holding that what I said was *true*."[2] Yet the fundamental question in the whole debate concerns the *truth* of the resurrection.

In particular, how are we to *interpret* the teaching of the New Testament and indeed *reinterpret* it in a way that makes sense to the twentieth-century mind? This task is indispensable. Moreover, as the Archbishop of Canterbury put it in the summer of 1984, it has long been accepted that "within the Church of England there may be *some variety of interpretation* over the various tenets of the Faith." That too is a fact. The media got hold of this well, for newscasters have kept saying that the controversy was about "the interpretation of the church's teaching." They were right.

But what are the limits of legitimate reinterpretation? To "interpret" means to explain the meaning of something by translating it either into another language or into more familiar and therefore more intelligible terms. Before the meaning of any words or events can be ex-

plained, therefore, their original meaning has to be determined. This is the first responsibility for interpreters. They
have no liberty to *change* the meaning; their job is to
*discover* and then *elucidate* it. So interpreters begin their
task by seeking to penetrate the mind of the writer or
speaker whom they are to interpret. What did he mean?
How did he intend his readers or hearers to understand
him? For this is the *sensus literalis,* the author's plain and
obvious meaning, as opposed to allegorical or other fan-
ciful ideas which less conscientious interpreters read into
him. In the succinct words of Professor E. D. Hirsch, "a
text means what its author meant."[3] It is a principle which
applies to all documents, whether biblical, literary or legal.

Even Rudolf Bultmann seems to have implied this in
his "demythologizing" program. He kept repeating in *Kerygma and Myth* (1953) that "the real purpose of myth is
to express. . . ." Whose purpose was he talking about? If
he meant that it was the biblical authors' self-conscious
intention to use myth in order to convey truths which
they could not express in any other way, and if he was
right about their purpose, then I would myself have no
difficulty about demythologizing or remythologizing; for
it would be an essential part of the interpreter's task.

If, however, the apostles were not deliberately using a
mythical framework, but were rather intending to describe events which they believed to be both historically
true and theologically significant (for example, when they
wrote about Jesus being born of a virgin or resurrected
from death), then we have no right to demythologize
their testimony, attempting to preserve the theology

while rejecting the history; for this would not be to reinterpret them, but to contradict them.

So the fundamental question is this: to what were the apostles bearing witness when they spoke and wrote about Jesus' resurrection? David Jenkins has said, "I believe in the Resurrection, in exactly the same sense as St. Paul believed in the Resurrection." That is a good statement. It presumably means that, if the bishop were to become convinced that Paul believed in a historical and physical event, then he would believe it too. What then did the apostles believe and teach?

The apostle Peter, according to Luke in the Acts, certainly believed that Jesus' resurrection resulted in an empty tomb. For in his sermon on the Day of Pentecost, quoting from Psalm 16, he said that he "was not abandoned to the grave, nor did his body see decay" (Acts 2:31). The four Gospel writers also bear witness to this, and the first evangelist relates the story that the guards were bribed by the priests to spread the rumor that "his disciples came during the night and stole him away while we were asleep." It would have been necessary to invent this yarn only if the body had disappeared (Mt 28:11-15).

Did Paul believe in the empty tomb? Some scholars follow Bultmann and insist that he did not, and they make much capital out of his supposed ignorance of it. They are surely mistaken, however. Consider Paul's statement of the gospel in 1 Corinthians 15:

> Now, brothers, I want to remind you of the gospel I preached to you, which you received and on which you have taken your stand. By this gospel you are saved, if you hold firmly to the word I preached to you.

Otherwise, you have believed in vain. For what I received I passed on to you as of first importance: that Christ died for our sins according to the Scriptures, that he was buried, that he was raised on the third day according to the Scriptures, and that he appeared . . . (vv. 1-5)

Before we examine the content of this gospel, it is noteworthy that Paul declares it to be both the *original* and the *universal* gospel. It was the original gospel in the sense that, far from inventing or ever formulating it himself, Paul says he had "received" it from others and had passed it on to the Corinthians. Since his statement of it is in essence the same as that preached by Peter in the early chapters of the Acts, it seems probable that Paul had "received" it from Peter on his first visit to Jerusalem two or three years after his conversion. It was therefore the original gospel and had become the gospel of the universal church. Paul insists on this as he concludes his statement: "whether, then, it was I [Paul] or they [the Jerusalem apostles], this is what we [the apostles] preach, and this is what you [Corinthian Christians] believed" (v. 11). The four pronouns "I," "they," "we," "you" clearly express universality. All the apostles preached the same gospel, and all the believers had received it.

As for the content of this original and universal apostolic gospel, it consisted of four successive events. First, "Christ died for our sins according to the Scriptures," so that his death was a historical event, with saving significance, foretold in the Old Testament. Second, "he was buried," which is not elaborated. Third, "he was raised on the third day according to the Scriptures," so that his resurrection was a divine act (not "he rose" but "he was raised"), a historical event ("on the third day") and also foretold in the Old Testament. Fourth, "he appeared" or "he was seen." Paul then proceeds to list the six main official resurrection appearances: three to individual apostles (Peter, James and himself), two to the group of apostles and one to more than five hundred at the same time, the majority of whom were still alive and were therefore able to testify.

At first it seems that Paul lists the four events (Jesus' death, burial, resurrection and appearances) as if they were of equal importance. On second reading, however, it becomes clear that he focuses on two—the death and resurrection—and adds the other two—the burial and the appearances—to demonstrate their historicity. Thus "Christ died" and (to prove the reality of his death) "he was buried." Again, "he was raised" and (to prove the reality of his resurrection) "he appeared" to certain chosen witnesses. In this way his burial attested his death (for, although occasionally people have been buried alive, the purpose of burial is to dispose of a corpse), and his appearances attested his resurrection (for, if he had not been raised objectively, he could not have been seen objectively).

**Datable and Physical**
Two truths about the resurrection stand out from this statement of the gospel. First, it was *datable*. For God raised Jesus "on the third day." This apparently insignificant detail was part of the apostolic gospel and later became incorporated in the Apostles' Creed ("on the

third day he rose again"). In this respect it is rather similar to that other clause "suffered under Pontius Pilate." Together these clauses indicate that both the crucifixion and the resurrection were datable historical events. Moreover, the preservation of the words "on the third day" are the more remarkable because all four evangelists write that the resurrection was discovered (and presumably happened) "on the first day of the week"; it shows the independence of "the Easter reports" (in the Gospels) from "the Easter kerygma" (in Paul's Epistle).[4] This reference to the third day makes me wonder how David Jenkins in the televised *Credo* program already mentioned could have said that, even from reading Paul in 1 Corinthians, it did not seem to him that "there was any one event which you could identify with the Resurrection"—only "a series of experiences." But on the contrary, although there was indeed a series of experiences (namely, the appearances of the risen Lord), which lasted forty days (Acts 1:3), there was a particular event (the resurrection) which gave rise to them, which took place on the third day and to which the church's continuing Sunday worship bears witness.

Second, the resurrection event was *physical* as well as *datable*. That is, it involved the body of Jesus. The four events (the death, burial, resurrection and appearances) must be taken together. The four verbs have the same subject (Christ) and surely concern his body. When Paul wrote "Christ died . . . and was buried," he was certainly referring to his body. When therefore he continued "he was raised and he appeared," the natural interpretation is that Paul was still referring to his body. What possible

warrant is there to change the subject in the middle of the
statement and say that, though the death and burial were
physical, the resurrection and appearances were spiritual?
No, it is the same Lord Jesus who died and was buried,
who then was raised and seen.

True, when the dead and buried body of Jesus was
raised, it was changed in the process. It is incredible that
Bultmann could dismiss the resurrection by alluding to it
as "the resuscitation of a corpse." It is also regrettable that
David Jenkins said the resurrection was "more than a
conjuring trick with bones," since, he thought, this is the
way orthodox believers conceive of it. We emphatically
do not, however. The "raising" of Jesus' body involved
the changing of it. Nevertheless, his body was involved.
When Paul wrote that Jesus died, was buried and was
raised, he assuredly did not mean that he was raised *while
still remaining buried.* That would make nonsense of the
apostle's declaration. As Earle Ellis has written, it is extremely unlikely that the earliest Palestinian Christians
could have conceived some kind of "spiritual" resurrection: "To them an *anastasis* (resurrection) without an
empty grave would have been about as meaningful as a
square circle."[5] Paul was affirming, then, that what was
"raised" was precisely what had been "buried," namely,
the Lord's body, and that therefore the tomb was empty.
Luke records him as preaching the same four events in
Pisidian Antioch: "They asked Pilate to have him executed. . . . They took him down from the tree and laid him
in a tomb. But God raised him from the dead, and for
many days he was seen . . ." He then added that this act
of God in raising Jesus meant that his body "did not see

decay" (Acts 13:28-31, 37).

## Does It Matter?

If the first question about the resurrection was "Is it true?" the second is "Does it matter?" Why should we be so concerned to show that Paul's gospel of the resurrection referred to a datable event which involved for Jesus a transformed body and an empty tomb? Why not be satisfied with David Jenkins's statement that he believes in Jesus' "resurrection" in the sense that he believes in his "risenness"? Why is that not enough?

It is not enough, first, because it is not what the apostles believed and proclaimed. This is the issue of truth. It is also not enough because, second, it could not have secured the results which the apostles say Jesus' resurrection did secure. The resurrection, they declared, radically changed their past, their present and their future. How?

Take their past first. It is hard for us to grasp, let alone to feel, how completely the verdict seemed to have gone against Jesus when he died, and how in consequence the apostles' past hopes had been extinguished. Jesus had been condemned in a Jewish court for blasphemy by duly authorized legal procedures. He was then sentenced and executed for sedition by the Romans. Worse, he had been "hanged on a tree" and therefore (according to Deut 21:22-23) had died under the curse of God. After that he was taken down from the cross and buried, which was the final touch in disposing of him. The public rejection of Jesus could not have been more thorough. At every dimension he was finished—judicial, political, spiritual and physical. Religion, law, God, man and death had all conspired to wipe him off the face of the earth. It was all over now. The verdict was as decisive as it could possibly have been. No power on earth could ever rescue or reinstate him.

But the apostles had not taken into account the resurrection power of God. Small wonder that their earliest proclamation could be summarized in the words "you killed him, but God raised him." And in raising him, God reversed the verdict which had been passed on him. The apostles expressed this dramatic reversal in different ways. For example, "God has made this Jesus, whom you crucified, both Lord and Christ" (Acts 2:36). Again, God "raised Jesus from the dead—whom you had killed by hanging him on a tree. God exalted him to his own right hand as Prince and Savior that he might give repentance and forgiveness of sins to Israel" (Acts 5:30-31). And again, he "was declared with power to be the Son of God by his resurrection from the dead" (Rom 1:4). In other words, by raising Jesus, God was making a declaration about him and in particular was turning all human opinions about him upside-down. Condemned for blasphemy, he was now designated Son of God by the resurrection. Executed for sedition for claiming to be a king, God made him "both Lord and Christ." Hanged on a tree under the curse of God, he was vindicated as the Savior of sinners, the curse he bore being due to us and not to him.

To their repeated statement "you killed him, but God raised him," the apostles invariably added "and we are witnesses." They saw the resurrection neither as the survival of Jesus, nor as the recovery of their own temporarily lost morale, but as a deliberate, divine act by which God raised him from death and so reversed the verdict of humanity. Moreover, since the verdict passed on Jesus by his condemnation and crucifixion was public, the reversal of it by resurrection had to be public too. That is why after he was raised he appeared. There had to be witnesses who could testify, on the basis of the objective evidence that the tomb was empty and the Lord was seen, that God had raised him from the dead.

## A Transforming Power

The resurrection of Jesus transformed the *present* for the apostles, as well as the past. For they saw it as an objective, historical demonstration of God's power, and they knew that the same power was available for them. In the Old Testament the chief proof of God's power was the creation. Jeremiah could say to Yahweh: "Sovereign LORD, you have made the heavens and the earth by your great power and outstretched arm. Nothing is too hard for you" (Jer 32:17).

But in New Testament days believers see the resurrection rather than the creation as the supreme manifestation of divine power. For death is our "last enemy." Medical and surgical skills can postpone it, but they cannot prevent it. In resurrecting Jesus, however, God's power accomplished what no human power could or can. He not only arrested the natural process of decomposition; he transcended it by raising Jesus to a new and incorruptible life over which death is impotent. So when Paul wanted the Ephesians to know God's "incomparably great power" which was at their disposal to save them, he not only prayed that their inward eyes might be enlightened to see it, but also directed their attention to the outward and objective display of God's power which he had "exerted in Christ when he raised him from the dead" (Eph 1:20). For the Christian's life is lived in "the power of his resurrection" (Phil 3:10). It begins when God raises us from the "death" of alienation from him and continues as he subdues our passions, transforms our character and even invigorates our bodies with Christ's risen life (2 Cor 4:10-11).

Thus we are given in Scripture two major paradigms of the power of God, the creation of the universe and the resurrection of Jesus. In Romans Paul even brings them together, describing the living God as the One "who gives life to the dead and calls things that are not as though they were" (4:17). In other words, God's power has been put forth above all in, first, creation out of nothing and, second, resurrection out of death. And both are objective and historical displays of power; for creation and resurrection have happened in time, and their results are visible. Otherwise they would not do as demonstrations of power. God's invisible power is clearly seen in what he has made (Rom 1:20). Similarly, although nobody saw the resurrection take place (anymore than anybody saw the creation), yet the risen Lord himself was seen, heard and touched (1 Jn 1:1) so that the chosen eyewitnesses were able to testify to what they had seen and heard.

## A Reason to Hope

The apostles' *future* was also transformed, as the resurrection became the ground of their hope. They saw it as the pledge—indeed the beginning—of God's new creation. Believers today have the same hope and the same basis for their hope. We have been "born again unto a living hope," as the apostle Peter declared. How so? "Through the resurrection of Jesus Christ from the dead" (1 Pet 1:3). The reason we look forward with confidence to the consummation of all things is that we look back with confidence to the resurrection. The Christian hope has already begun to be fulfilled. Eschatology has already begun to be realized. Already we are living in the last days, for they were inaugurated by Jesus and in particular by his resurrection.

The Christian hope focuses on the resurrection of the body and the regeneration of the universe, both of which the New Testament promises at the *eschaton.*

In the Apostles' Creed we affirm our belief in *two* resurrections, namely, Christ's and ours. And the former is the pledge of the latter, the "first fruits" of the final harvest (1 Cor 15:20). If his resurrection did not entail the raising and changing of his body, we would have to erase the penultimate clause of the Creed in which we declare our belief in "the resurrection of *the body.*" Mind you, this needs to be understood. The resurrection of Jesus was not, and our resurrection will not be, a resuscitation. Resurrection and resuscitation are two quite different things. Lazarus, the daughter of Jairus and the son of the widow of Nain were all resuscitated by Jesus. That is, they were brought back to this life. In consequence they have our sympathy, as C. S. Lewis once put it, because they then "had all their dying to do again."[6] But Jesus rose in a transformed body, to die no more. Indeed, "he cannot die again; death no longer has mastery over him" (Rom 6:9; compare Rev 1:18).

Our resurrection bodies will be like the resurrection body of Jesus, Paul assures us. "Just as we have borne the likeness of the earthly man [Adam], so shall we bear the likeness of the man from heaven [Christ]" (1 Cor 15:49); for when Christ comes he "will transform our lowly bodies so that they will be like his glorious body" (Phil 3:21). Our resurrection bodies will not, then, be miraculously reconstituted out of the particles of which they are at present composed. That notion is absurd. Neither the Bible nor the church has ever taught it, even if some individual Christians may have believed it. To be sure, it seems that in creating our resurrection bodies God will use whatever remains of our present bodies, as he did in the case of Jesus, but they will be new bodies invested with new powers. To illustrate the change, Paul used the picture of seeds and flowers (1 Cor 15:35-38). As each flower grows from its own seed, yet is gloriously different from it in size, color, shape and scent, so will it be with our resurrection bodies. There will be some continuity (as between seed and flower), but more striking still will be the discontinuity.

The apostle goes on to list four contrasts between our two bodies (vv. 42-44). This body is "perishable" (its life limited to a few decades); the new will be "imperishable" (subject to neither disease, nor decay, nor death). This body "is sown in dishonor" (not that there is anything dishonorable about our bodies in themselves, but that their appetites have been perverted by sin); it will be "raised in glory" (all our selfish passions having been eradicated). Third, our present body is marked by "weakness" (written all over it are the words "Fragile—Handle with Care"); our new body will be characterized by "power" (it will have a different metabolism and will no longer be subject to the same limitations of time and space, as we see in the resurrection body of Jesus). Fourth, we now have "a natural body" (the vehicle of natural, earthly, physiological life), whereas one day we will have "a spiritual body" (still a real body, but adapted to spiritual life and the vehicle of our redeemed personality). Thus, the Christian hope is not the immortality of the soul (a shadowy, disembodied existence), but the resurrection of the body (a perfect instrument for the expression of our new life).

The Christian hope is not limited to the "redemption" (Rom 8:23) and transformation of our individual bodies, however. The universe is to be redeemed and transformed. Already in the Old Testament we read of God's intention to "create new heavens and a new earth" (Is 65:17). Similarly, Jesus spoke of "the renewal of all things" (literally, the "regeneration" or "the new birth" of the world—Mt 19:28), while Peter referred to the final "restoration" of everything (Acts 3:21). Similarly, Paul wrote that nature itself will one day be delivered from its bondage to decay, and that the pains of the present order will prove to be the birthpangs of the new (Rom 8:18-25). And in his great vision which concludes the New Testament John caught a glimpse of "a new heaven and a new earth," and of the "new Jerusalem" which, though it is seen "coming down out of heaven from God" as his creation and gift, will nevertheless be adorned with the "glory and honor" which the nations and their leaders will bring into it (Rev 21:1-2, 26; compare 2 Pet 3:13).

So then, the living hope of the New Testament is an impressively "material" expectation for both the individual and the cosmos. For the individual believer it is not survival merely, nor even immortality, but a resurrected body. For the cosmos it will not be an ethereal "heaven," but a regenerated universe. And of these two expectations the resurrection of Jesus is the ground. It provides solid, visible, public evidence of God's purpose to complete what he has begun, to redeem nature, to give us new bodies in a new world.

## A Futile Faith

Although the Bishop of Durham says he believes in the resurrection of Jesus, we must now conclude that he does not, or at least not in the sense in which the apostles believed and proclaimed it. For they were bearing witness to an event which was simultaneously datable, historical, physical and supernatural. Only by such an objective act of God could he publicly vindicate the rejected and crucified Jesus, demonstrate the greatness of his power and prove to us that his new creation had begun.

So why do Bishop Jenkins and some others set aside the apostles' gospel of the resurrection, which was both the original and the universal faith of the church and which the postapostolic church has continued to maintain in a virtually uninterrupted tradition? They cannot argue that the apostles were writing "myth," whose purpose was to describe not historical events but a transcendent reality, for they were bearing witness to the life, death, burial, resurrection and appearances of Jesus as a historical and significant sequence. We have no liberty therefore to dissolve it into a "meaning" which is not historical. Nor can skeptics complain that nobody has ever seen a resurrection and that therefore it must be pronounced unscientific since science can handle only observable phenomena of the present. But of course so far there has been only one resurrection, because the resurrection of Jesus was unique. Any claim that other resurrections have taken place would constitute a great problem to Christian faith; their absence is no problem at all.

So I repeat my question: why are those who doubt or deny the bodily resurrection of Jesus making such a song and dance about it? It can only be that their view of the universe precludes *a priori* the possibility of miracles. Yet this is exceedingly strange since (a) it leads them to con-tradict the apostles' gospel and the church's tradition, (b) it is a secular, not a Christian, viewpoint, (c) there are many distinguished scientists (as we have seen) who find no dichotomy betwen their scientific world view and their acceptance of the possibility of miracle, and (d) a Jewish scholar like Professor Pinchas Lapide, though he does not accept Jesus' Messiahship, has written a book entitled *The Resurrection of Jesus* (1984) in which he rejects the skepticism of Christian theologians and de-ploys powerful arguments for its historicity.

Nobody has summed up more eloquently than Paul the dire consequences of denying the resurrection of Jesus in the historical, physical sense in which he proclaimed it. If Christ has not been raised from the dead, he wrote, then the apostles were false witnesses, their preaching and our faith are alike futile, we are still in our sins, the Christian dead have perished, and the Christian living are to be pitied more than anybody else (1 Cor 15:14-18).

## For Further Reading

J. N. D. Anderson, *Evidence for the Resurrection* (IVP, 1950).

Michael Green, *The Day Death Died* (IVP, 1982).

G. E. Ladd, *I Believe in the Resurrection of Jesus* (Eerdmans, 1975).

# 5
# THE VIRGIN
# BIRTH

*B*ishop David Jenkins also doubts, and even appears to deny, the historical reality of the virgin birth. He has referred to "the symbolic and mythological nature of the story of the Virgin birth."[1] In his diocesan letter for December 1984 he wrote that some people either "simply cannot understand, or simply will not listen to, the point that many of the stories of the Bible are 'for real', not by being literally true, but by being inspired symbols of a living faith about the real activity of God."

But many of the bishop's critics are neither as ignorant nor as obstinate as he suggests. We know very well that there is a literary genre called "myth" which sets out to present truth in historical form without claiming that it is historical. That is not in dispute between us. Many pagan myths were current in the first century, including one of Greek and Egyptian origin about a savior-god born of a virgin mother who ruled both sky and sea. But these stories were self-evidently myths. People did not believe they were historical. The question is whether the evangelists were deliberately writing myth when they told the story of the virgin birth and whether they intended us to understand it as such. My answer is "definitely not." Professor Henry Chadwick was right in a recent article to point out that the Apostles' Creed includes both "historical" and "poetic" statements. "He sits at the right hand of God" belongs to the latter category, but "he was born of the Virgin Mary" and "the third day he rose again from the dead" to the former.

It is true that Jesus' birth of a virgin does not receive as much emphasis in the New Testament as his death and resurrection. None of Peter's early speeches in the Acts nor Paul's summary of the gospel in 1 Corinthians 15 contains an allusion to the virgin birth. Although the four evangelists are indeed writing what Mark called "the gospel about Jesus Christ" (Mk 1:1), and although Matthew and Luke in their Gospels do record the virgin birth, yet nowhere else in the New Testament could it be said to be integral to the good news. Nevertheless, it is plainly taught in the Gospels mentioned and has been the virtually unanimous belief of the universal church ever since. This teaching and tradition cannot lightly be set aside. Besides, it is entirely congruous that a supernatural person (who was simultaneously God and man) should enter as well as leave the world in a supernatural way.

Attacks on the virgin birth are not new. On the contrary,

they are as old as Christianity itself. In the first century both the Jewish Ebionites and certain Gnostic sects denied the deity of Jesus and therefore went on to dismiss the story of his virgin birth. In the second century, the heretic Marcion, who completely rejected the Old Testament, published a version of one Gospel only (Luke's) which omitted its first two chapters. Since then the skeptics and rationalists of every century have disputed or dismissed the virgin birth. For example, Renan the French humanist, whose *Vie de Jésus* created a sensation when it was published in 1863, began his second chapter: "Jesus was born at Nazareth, a small town of Galilee, which before his time had no celebrity. . . . His father Joseph and his mother Mary were people in humble circumstances." These critics, however, were outside the church.

What is new today is that their views are tolerated inside, even among church leaders who have solemnly undertaken to guard and teach the historic Christian faith. At the beginning of this century William Temple's ordination was postponed for two years until he was sure about Jesus' virgin birth and bodily resurrection, and in 1917 and 1918 Archbishop Randall Davidson declined to consecrate Hensley Henson, who had been nominated Bishop of Hereford, until he was able to give satisfactory assurances that he was not denying these doctrines of the Creed. It is because Archbishop John Habgood proceeded with the consecration of David Jenkins without receiving similar assurances that many of us are disturbed by this grave precedent.

It may be wise at this point to clarify what is meant by the "virgin birth." It is a misleading expression, because it suggests that there was something unusual about Jesus' birth, whereas his birth was entirely normal and natural. It was his conception which was abnormal, indeed supernatural; for he was conceived by the operation of the Holy Spirit, without the cooperation of a human father.

As with the resurrection, so with our discussion of the virgin birth, there are two questions which need to be asked. The first concerns its historicity (did it happen?) and the second its significance (does it matter?).

## The Historicity of the Virgin Birth
As we weigh the historical evidence for the virgin birth, four factors should be taken into consideration. First, *the witness of the evangelists:* Matthew and Luke both bear an unambiguous witness to the virginity of Mary. True, they trace the genealogy of Jesus through Joseph and are uninhibited in referring to Joseph as Jesus' "father." But after he had married Mary, he *was* Jesus' legal father. So there is no difficulty here. The fact is that, according to both the first and the third evangelists, when Mary became pregnant she was betrothed not married to Joseph, and when Jesus was born she was still a virgin. Moreover, it is quite clear that Matthew and Luke believed this. They were writing prose not poetry, history not myth.

Some scholars argue that Matthew in particular (not Luke, whose claim to historical investigation has already been mentioned) was not intending to write a purely historical narrative, but that he freely expanded and embellished his sources so that the result was "midrash," that is, "a mixture of history and nonhistory," which (it is further said) was a familiar form of Jewish literature in his day. This suggestion is far from proven, however. Evidence is lacking in three critical areas: first, that it was a common literary genre at that time (it does not seem to have become so until the second century); second, that Matthew intended to write midrash (he certainly was not embroidering the Old Testament with fiction, which is what the midrashic commentators did); and third, that his contemporaries understood him to be using this particular form (the early church fathers did not).[2] Instead, as one reads Matthew's Gospel freshly, one is struck by the detailed historical context of people, places and dates in which he sets his story.

If it is conceded that Matthew and Luke believed that Mary the mother of Jesus was a virgin, why, it is asked, do Mark and John not say so too? And why is the rest of the New Testament silent about Jesus' virgin birth? In reply, we begin by remembering that the argument from silence is notoriously unreliable. For example, Mark and John tell us nothing about the childhood of Jesus either; but we do not conclude from this that Jesus never had one. Next, there is indirect evidence that John did know about and believe the virgin birth. I am not thinking only of his great affirmation that "the Word became flesh and lived . . . among us" (Jn 1:14), but also of the recurring statements that Jesus "came from above," "came down from heaven," "was sent by the Father," and "came into the world." Some supernatural intervention would have been necessary to make these things possible. The fact that Mark and John omitted the story of the virgin birth is actually irrelevant for the simple reason that they did not set out to write about Jesus' birth and infancy at all. They both chose to begin their narrative with John the Baptist. The significant point is that the only two evangelists who did intend to describe Jesus' birth both declared that he was born of a virgin.

The second factor to be considered is *the authenticity of the atmosphere* which the stories breathe. As we read the early chapters of Matthew and Luke, we are transported back into the final days of the Old Testament. Zechariah and Elizabeth, Joseph and Mary, Simeon and Anna are devout Old Testament believers who are looking and waiting for the kingdom of God. The context is steeped in Old Testament piety. The language, style and structure of the narratives are thoroughly Hebraic. Far from being later legendary accretions, these stories sound and feel as if they were written very early indeed.

In addition, the narrative unfolds with simplicity and discretion. It is true that there were pagan stories current of the gods having sexual intercourse with human women. But in place of those crude and fantastic myths, the evangelists are reticent; they treat the sacred intimacies of the conception of Jesus with the utmost delicacy.

Third, we need to ask about *the origin of the story* of the virgin birth. The narratives of Matthew and Luke share the same core. They both attribute Mary's pregnancy to the Holy Spirit not Joseph, and they both refer to the problems and perplexities which were caused by her virginity. But their accounts are clearly independent (there is no evidence of collusion) and complementary (they are told from different perspectives). Luke writes of the annunciation to Mary and of her perplexity as to how she could become a mother when she was not yet married.

Matthew, on the other hand, writes of Joseph's discovery of Mary's pregnancy and of his perplexity, his resolve to divorce her because the child was not his, and his dream in which God tells him to take her home as his wife. Thus Luke tells Mary's story, while Matthew tells Joseph's. Ultimately the facts must have come from Mary and Joseph themselves, whether in written or spoken form. During Luke's two and a half years of freedom in Palestine, to which I have already referred, there seems every possibility, even probability, that he met the Virgin Mary personally and received her story from her own lips. At all events, the internal evidence suggests that we have in the New Testament two genuine, early, separate accounts of the virgin birth, each independent of the other, and each supplementing the other, the one going back to Joseph and the other to Mary.

The fourth factor we need to ponder is *the rumor of Jesus' illegitimacy.* "The first and most indisputable fact about the birth of Jesus," wrote J. A. T. Robinson, "is that it occurred out of wedlock. The one option for which there is no evidence is that Jesus is the lawful son of Joseph and Mary. The only choice open to us is between a virgin birth and an illegitimate birth."[3]

It is clear that rumors of Jesus' possible illegitimacy were being spread during his public ministry in an attempt to discredit him. For example, when he declared that certain unbelieving Jews did not have Abraham as their father but the devil, they retorted "*We* are not illegitimate children," which sounds like an innuendo that he was (Jn 8:41). On another occasion, this time in his own hometown, when the people were offended by his teaching, they asked contemptuously, "Isn't this Mary's son?" (Mk 6:3). In a patriarchal society this was a deliberate insult; the insinuation would not have been missed. Then on a third occasion, unbelievers shouted at the man born blind, whom Jesus had healed: "We know that God spoke to Moses, but as for this fellow, we don't even know where he comes from" (Jn 9:29).

These rumors of Jesus' illegitimacy persisted long after his death. In the Jewish Talmud they became explicit. And in the third century the Christian scholar Origen had to answer the jibe of the critic Celsus that Joseph turned Mary out of his home because she had committed adultery with a soldier named Panthera.[4] How on earth could these hints and slanders have arisen unless it were known that Mary was already pregnant when Joseph married her? Distasteful as this gossip is, it is corroborative evidence of the virgin birth.

## The Significance of the Virgin Birth

We move now from the evidence for the historicity of the virgin birth to the question of its significance: does it matter? We have already noted that the birth of Jesus is not given the same prominence in the New Testament as is his resurrection, which is not in the least surprising, since his resurrection appearances were public and had eyewitnesses, whereas the virgin birth was essentially private and was not witnessed. Yet the vigor with which critics have attacked it suggests that they recognize its importance.

Here is Luke's account of the annunciation:

In the sixth month, God sent the angel Gabriel to

Nazareth, a town in Galilee, to a virgin pledged to be married to a man named Joseph, a descendant of David. The virgin's name was Mary. The angel went to her and said, "Greetings, you who are highly favored! The Lord is with you."

Mary was greatly troubled at his words and wondered what kind of greeting this might be. But the angel said to her, "Do not be afraid, Mary, you have found favor with God. You will be with child and give birth to a son, and you are to give him the name Jesus. He will be great and will be called the Son of the Most High. The Lord God will give him the throne of his father David, and he will reign over the house of Jacob forever; his kingdom will never end."

"How will this be," Mary asked the angel, "since I am a virgin?"

The angel answered, "The Holy Spirit will come upon you, and the power of the Most High will overshadow you. So the holy one to be born will be called the Son of God. Even Elizabeth your relative is going to have a child in her old age, and she who was said to be barren is in her sixth month. For nothing is impossible with God."

"I am the Lord's servant," Mary answered. "May it be to me as you have said." Then the angel left her. (Lk 1:26-36)

After the angel had greeted Mary as one who enjoyed God's special favor and presence, his disclosure to her of God's purpose was in two clear stages, which dovetail with one another. The first stressed her child's continuity with the past, because she would bear him. The second stressed his discontinuity, even his uniqueness, because the Holy Spirit would overshadow her.

In the first section (vv. 30-34) the angel announced that Mary would conceive and bear a son, that he would be "great" (being named both "Jesus" and "the Son of the Most High" in reference to his saving, Messianic ministry) and that he would occupy the throne of his father David and reign over the house of Jacob forever. In other words, he would inherit from his mother both his humanity ("you will . . . give birth to a son") and his title to the Messianic throne. At least this seems to be implied. Certainly the apostle Paul was later to emphasize it when writing that Jesus "as to his human nature was a descendant of David" (Rom 1:3).[5] At the same time, Joseph is explicitly described as being descended from David. By naming Jesus (Mt 1:21, 25), he accepted him as his son, and by accepting him, "conferred on him all the legal rights of legitimate sonship."[6]

In the second section (v. 35) the angel continued, saying that the Holy Spirit would come upon Mary and the creative power of the Most High would overshadow her (the cloud being in Scripture a symbol of God's presence). And "therefore" the child to be born of her would be unique, both "the holy one" (surely a reference to his sinlessness) and "the Son of God" (here evidently in a deeper sense than as a Messianic title).

In this way it was announced to Mary that her son's humanity and Messiahship would be derived from her, the mother who would conceive and bear him, while his sinlessness and deity would be derived from the Holy Spirit who would powerfully overshadow her. The continuity would be due to his natural birth by Mary, and the discontinuity to his supernatural conception by the Holy Spirit. He would be descended from Adam by his birth, but be constituted the Second Adam (the head of the new humanity) by his conception of the Holy Spirit.

As a result of the virgin birth (that is, of the truth of the Apostles' Creed that he was "conceived by the Holy Spirit, born of the Virgin Mary"), Jesus Christ was simultaneously Mary's son and God's Son, human and divine, the Messiah descended from David and the sinless Savior of sinners. Since God is free and sovereign and we have no liberty to circumscribe him, he could doubtless have secured this result by some other means. But the New Testament evidence is that he chose to do it by a virgin birth, and it is not difficult to understand its reasonableness and appropriateness.

Mary's response to the angelic announcement wins our immediate admiration. "I am the Lord's servant," she said. "May it be to me as you have said." Once God's purpose and method had been explained to her, she did not demur. She was entirely at his disposal. She expressed her total willingness to be the virgin mother of the Son of God. Of course it was an enormous privilege for her: "the Mighty One has done great things for me," she sang (Lk 1:49). Yet it was an awesome and costly responsibility too. It involved a readiness to become pregnant before she was married and so to expose herself to the shame and suffering of being thought an immoral woman. To me the humility and courage of Mary in submitting to the virgin birth stand out in contrast to the attitudes of the critics who deny it.

We need the humility of Mary. She accepted God's purpose, saying "May it be to me as you have said." But the
tendency of many today is to reject it because it does not
fit in with their presuppositions. Those who reject miracles in general and the virgin birth in particular because
they believe the universe to be a closed system, do not
seem to see the anomaly of dictating to the Creator what
he is permitted to do in his own creation. Would it not
be more modest to copy Mary's reaction of submissive-
ness to God's way?

We also need Mary's courage. She was so completely
willing for God to fulfill his purpose that she was ready
to risk the stigma of being an unmarried mother, of being
thought an adulteress herself and of bearing an illegitimate child. She surrendered her reputation to God's will.
I sometimes wonder if the major cause of much theological liberalism is that some scholars care more about their
reputation than about God's revelation. Finding it hard to
be ridiculed for being naive and credulous enough to
believe in miracles, they are tempted to sacrifice God's
revelation on the altar of their own respectability. I do not
say that they always do so. But I feel it right to make the
point because I have myself felt the strength of this temp-
tation. But *of course* critics will smirk and scoff: let them!
What matters is that we allow God to be God and to do
things his way, even if with Mary we thereby risk losing
our good name.

### For Further Reading
John Gresham Machen, *The Virgin Birth* (Baker, 1965).
James Orr, *The Virgin Birth of Christ* (Scribners, 1907).

# 6
# THE UNIQUENESS OF JESUS

$W$e move now to a different and more subtle threat to the traditional understanding of Christianity. It comes not from theological liberalism (which questions the authority of the New Testament witnesses) but from religious pluralism (which questions the uniqueness and finality of Jesus Christ). In the West this is a comparatively recent phenomenon and has resulted from a postwar immigration policy which encouraged the influx of people of other races and faiths. Today nearly a million Muslims live in the United Kingdom and over three million live in the United States. The second largest Hindu community in the world outside India (after Durban) is in Leicester, and there are Hindu temples in Birmingham and Wolverhampton, Manchester and Leeds, Coventry and Bristol, and numerous smaller towns. In Britain it is not unusual to see saffron-robed Buddhist monks in the streets, and turbaned Sikhs number about two hundred thousand.[1] Alongside adherents of these ancient religions are devotees of modern cults, whose origin is either Western (for example, Christian Scientists, Mormons and Jehovah's Witnesses) or Oriental (for example, Hare Krishna, the Divine Light Mission and other groups who practice yoga and transcendental meditation).

This situation has had a profound effect on many Westerners who had never before questioned their own, if they had any, religious commitment to Christianity. Previously other religions seemed to belong only to distant places and unread books, but now people see these religions being practiced in their own neighborhood, place of work and local school or college. The benefits are obvious. The comparative study of religions, which is an essential part of our education, has come to life. And cultural diversity enriches the quality of our experience, even if it also makes harmonious community relations more difficult.

## The Danger of Syncretism

How then are we to think of other religions? The word that immediately springs to most people's minds is *tolerance*, but they do not always stop to define what they mean by it. It may help if we distinguish between three kinds. The first may be called *legal* tolerance, which ensures that every minority's religious and political rights (usually summarized as the freedom to "profess, practice and propagate") are adequately protected in law. This is obviously right. Another kind is *social* tolerance, which encourages respect for all persons, whatever views they may hold, and seeks to understand and appreciate their position. This too is a virtue which Christians wish to cultivate; it arises naturally from our recognition that all human beings are God's creation and bear his image, and that we are meant to live together in amity. But what about *intellectual* tolerance, which is the third kind? To cultivate a mind so broad that it can tolerate every opinion, without ever detecting anything in it to reject, is not a virtue; it is the vice of the feeble-minded. It can degenerate into an unprincipled confusion of truth with error, and goodness with evil. Christians, who believe that truth and goodness have been revealed in Christ, cannot possibly come to terms with it.

In the extreme form I have just described, intellectual tolerance is rare. A much more popular expression of it is syncretism, by which is meant the reconciliation or fusion of different religious beliefs into a single harmonious system. W. A. Visser't Hooft, a former general secretary of the World Council of Churches, has given this fuller definition of syncretism. It is "the view . . . that there is no unique revelation in history, that there are many different ways to reach the divine reality, that all formulations of religious truth or experience are by their very nature inadequate expressions of that truth, and that it is necessary to harmonize as much as possible all religious ideas and experiences, so as to create one universal religion for mankind."[2] Dr. Visser't Hooft goes on to show how the shrinkage of the modern world, the search for the unity of the human race and the distaste for religious controversy have combined to make syncretism very appealing.

The natural home of syncretism is India, and its greatest exponent has probably been the nineteenth-century Hindu mystic, Ramakrishna Paramahamsa. After years of study "he reached the conclusion that all religions in their inmost content are one." [3] He was followed by Swami Vivekananda, the main founder of the Ramakrishna Mission, which teaches that all religions are paths to the one Supreme Reality. Indian influence is clearly traceable in the Theosophical Society, founded in New York in 1875 mainly by Madame H. P. Blavatsky; its best-known leader Annie Besant taught that Jesus was one incarnation "in a long list of outstanding spiritual Great Ones."[4] It was in nineteenth-century Muslim Iran, however, that the Bahai faith emerged (founded by Baha'ullah), which also stresses the essential unity of all religions.

So the spirit of syncretism is not confined to Asia. It has moved steadily westward and has recently seeped into some of the thinking of the World Council of Churches and its member churches. On Commonwealth Day in May 1966, for instance, a "multifaith service" was held in the church of St. Martin-in-the-Fields in London. In it Hindus, Buddhists, Muslims and Christians took part on equal terms, making four affirmations of a supposedly common faith, giving four readings from their respective Scriptures, and pronouncing four blessings, in only one of which the name of Jesus was mentioned for the first and last time. The secular press, of course, were enthusiastic and hailed it as "a significant milestone in religious history." In the Christian press, however, it was called "a betrayal of the

Christian faith," and that autumn in the Canterbury Con-
vocation the motion was carried by an overwhelming majority "that this house views with concern the holding of
multireligious services in Christian churches." Yet similar
services are still being arranged from time to time.

Then in 1984 the "Inter-Faith Consultative Group" of
the Church of England General Synod's Board for Mission
and Unity produced a report entitled *Towards a Theology
for Inter-Faith Dialogue*. After turning away from two op-
posite extremes, the one rejecting all dialogue and the
other all mission and evangelism (para. 15), the report
describes three possible positions, which it labels "exclusivism," "inclusivism" and "pluralism," although it
adds that each contains a range of views. "Exclusivism"
emphasizes the uniqueness of Christ as the only Savior,
the discontinuity between Christianity and other religions, and the primacy of evangelism (paras. 16-17). "Inclusivism" emphasizes that, although Jesus remains "nor-
mative," yet God's saving power is not confined to him;
other peoples receive salvation, and other religions are
forerunners of the gospel (paras. 18-19). "Pluralism" emphasizes that the different religions are culturally determined responses to God's revelation and wants other religions "brought into some kind of larger ecumenical
relationship where the truths of each are seen as complementary to each other" (paras. 20-21).

It is a disappointing document, not least in its biblical
section (paras. 24-59). A thorough and judicious critique
of it by Christopher Wright appeared in *Anvil* (vol. 1, no.
3, 1984). The report does not take with anything like
sufficient seriousness the biblical rejection of syncretism,

both its Old Testament polemic against idolatry and its New Testament affirmations (in the midst of a Greco-Roman world which was completely syncretistic) of the absolute uniqueness of Jesus. "The tragedy of syncretism," wrote Visser't Hooft, "is that, while it seeks to advance beyond the historical religions, it leads in fact to a regression."[5] That is, in order to achieve a reconciliation of religions, it is obliged to jettison the distinctives of each which are mutually irreconcilable. "It is high time," he went on, "that Christians should rediscover that the very heart of their faith is that Jesus Christ did not come to make a contribution to the religious storehouse of mankind, but that in him God reconciled the world unto himself."[6]

## Incarnation, Atonement, Resurrection

Bishop Lesslie Newbigin has clarified that we "do not claim finality for Christianity in any of its empirical manifestations"; instead, we "claim finality for Christ."[7] For as Bishop Stephen Neill has written, "the old saying 'Christianity is Christ' is almost exactly true."[8] If then the uniqueness of Christianity is the uniqueness of Christ, wherein does his uniqueness lie? Historically speaking, it is found in his birth, death and resurrection. As for his birth, he was conceived by the Holy Spirit, born of the Virgin Mary," and therefore is both God and man. As for his death, he died for our sins, in our place, to secure our salvation. As for his resurrection, he thereby conquered death and possesses universal authority. Or, to express these historical events theologically, the uniqueness of Jesus lies in the incarnation, the atonement and the exaltation. Each is unparalleled.

We begin with the incarnation of God in Jesus Christ.
God's eternal Word or Son "became flesh," taking to himself the fullness of our humanity. As a human being he
lived for a while on earth. In consequence, people saw
his glory, and in seeing him they saw the Father (Jn 1:14,
18; 14:9). Thus the Father gave to the world in and
through his incarnate Son a unique historical revelation
of himself.

Jews of course reject this. So do Muslims, since Muhammad in the Koran, misrepresenting it in grossly physical
terms, repudiated the idea that Allah should ever beget a
son. In Hinduism, however, many so-called avatars (meaning "descents," though often rendered "incarnations")
are claimed. The most celebrated are the incarnations of
Vishnu in Rama and Krishna. In the *Bhagavad Gita* Krishna tells Arjuna that he frequently takes human form: "I
have been born many times, Arjuna. . . . Although I am
unborn, everlasting, and I am the Lord of all, I come to
my realm of nature and through my wondrous power I
am born."[9] Perhaps even more striking was the claim of
Ramakrishna, who spoke of himself as "the same soul that
had been born before as Rama, as Krishna, as Jesus, or as
Buddha, born again as Ramakrishna."[10]

But incarnation and reincarnation are two fundamentally
different concepts. Not only are the Indian claims historically dubious, but they speak of multiple rebirths, each
of which was only temporary. The Christian affirmation,
by contrast, is that in Jesus of Nazareth God took human
flesh once and for all and forever. The incarnation was a
historical and unrepeatable event with permanent conse-

quences. Reigning at God's right hand today is the man
Christ Jesus, still human as well as divine, though now his
humanity has been glorified. Having assumed our human
nature, he has never discarded it, and he never will.

Second is the atonement. Startling as it may sound, the
incarnation was with a view to the atonement; his birth
was with a view to his death. The very name *Jesus* bears
witness to the salvation of God which he came to achieve.
For Christianity is in its very essence a rescue religion, and
the rescue was accomplished at enormous cost. The gospel tells of a loving God who refused either to condone
our sins or to visit them upon us, who took the initiative
to come after us and who pursued us even to the desolate
shame and agony of the cross. There God in Christ took
our place, bore our sins, suffered our penalty, and died
our death, in order that we might be forgiven, reconciled
and re-created.

There is nothing even approaching this in other religions. "If any other religion has anything in the least like
the doctrines of incarnation and atonement," wrote Bishop Stephen Neill, "I have yet to find it."[11] But it cannot
be found; Emil Brunner was right to refer to "the self-con-
fident optimism of all non-Christian religion," whereas in
the gospel the whole emphasis is on the gracious
"self-movement" of God toward sinners and on self-despair as "the antechamber of faith."[12]

Buddhism sees the human predicament in suffering
rather than sin and in "desire" which it teaches is the root
of suffering. Deliverance comes only through the aboli-
tion of desire by self-effort. There is no God and no savior. "Strive without ceasing" were the Buddha's last words

before he died. Philosophical Hinduism locates the problem in *maya,* usually understood as the "illusion" of our
space-time experience. Popular Hinduism, on the other
hand, teaches the inflexible doctrine of *karma:* each person must eat the fruit of their own wrongdoings, for
which there is no forgiveness, in an endless cycle *(sam-
sara)* of reincarnations, from which there is no escape.
Islam does indeed proclaim at the head of every *surah*
(chapter) of the Koran that Allah is compassionate and
merciful. Yet it discloses no costly historical display of his
mercy, and on closer inspection he is seen to be merciful
to the meritorious, to those who pray and give alms and
fast. The Koran has no message for sinners who deserve
nothing from God except judgment and who have no
merit to plead. Its symbol is the scales, standing for the
weighing of merit against demerit, not the cross, which
speaks only of grace, of God's free and unmerited favor
to sinners. In different ways and with different emphases
all the religions of the world proclaim the possibility of
self-salvation by self-reliance or the accumulation of merit; only the gospel proclaims salvation through the merit
of Another, who paid the price of sin in a unique, historical act of self-sacrifice.

Third, the resurrection is unique. There have been a
number of resuscitations. Three are attributed to Jesus in
the Gospels, two to the apostles in the Acts (one to Peter
and the other to Paul), and others have been claimed
during the history of the postapostolic church. But there
has been only one resurrection, namely, that of Jesus
Christ. By it God vindicated Jesus, defeated death and
inaugurated his new creation. In addition, Jesus' resurrec-

tion from death was the prelude to, even the beginning of, his exaltation as Lord. The "right hand of God" is a readily intelligible symbol of the place of supreme honor and authority. Because of his preeminent honor, his "name . . . above every name" (Phil 2:9), Jesus Christ is to be worshiped. Because of his preeminent authority, he is able to save, forgiving our sins and bestowing his Spirit upon us (Acts 2:33, 38). Moreover, the distinctive ministry of the Holy Spirit today is exercised in relation to Christ, as he himself foretold. The Spirit "glorifies" Christ, making his glory known (Jn 16:14-15). The Spirit "bears witness" to Christ so that people believe in him (Jn 15:26). The Spirit universalizes Christ, making him available to everybody everywhere (Jn 16:7). The Spirit makes Christ's indwelling within us a personal reality (Jn 14:17; Rom 8:9; Eph 3:16-19).

No comparable claims are made, or could be sustained, on behalf of the great religious leaders of the world. Although Hindus talk of "the Lord Krishna" and Buddhists of "the Lord Buddha," they do not mean what we mean by "the Lord Jesus." For, to be sure, "there are many 'gods' and many 'lords' . . . yet for us there is but one God, the Father, from whom all things came and for whom we live; and there is but one Lord, Jesus Christ, through whom all things came and through whom we live" (1 Cor 8:5-6). It is perhaps the combination of the "all things" (the universe) and the "we" (individual persons) that is most striking in this statement. Our claim is that the Lord Jesus both had a unique role in the creation of the universe and has a unique place in his followers' lives. The Buddhist does not claim to know the Buddha, nor the Confucianist

Confucius, nor the Muslim Muhammad, nor the Marxist Marx. Each reveres the founder of his religion or ideology as a great teacher of the past. Christians also look to Jesus as their teacher, but he is to us far more than that. We do claim to know him, as the Spirit makes him known to us. We dare even to echo Paul: "I consider everything a loss compared to the surpassing greatness of knowing Christ Jesus my Lord, for whose sake I have lost all things. I consider them rubbish, that I may gain Christ and be found in him" (Phil 3:8-9).

This, then, is the threefold uniqueness of Jesus Christ. Historically it lies in his birth, death and resurrection, and theologically in his incarnation, atonement and exaltation. Indeed, because in no other person but the historic Jesus of Nazareth has God become man and lived a human life on earth, died to bear the penalty of our sins, and been raised from death and exalted to glory, there is no other Savior, since there is no other person who is qualified to save. We must therefore give full weight to, and not attempt to tone down, the great New Testament affirmations of the uniqueness and finality of Jesus. "I am the way and the truth and the life. No one comes to the Father except through me" (Jn 14:6). "Salvation is found in no one else, for there is no other name under heaven given to men by which we must be saved" (Acts 4:12). "There is one God and one mediator between God and men, the man Christ Jesus, who gave himself as a ransom for all men" (1 Tim 2:5-6). Only one way, only one name, only one mediator. The claim is exclusive; it carries with it the negative corollary that "no one comes to the Father" except through Christ, and that there is "salvation . . . in no one else," since only he is the God-man, who gave himself as a ransom for men and can therefore be the mediator between God and men.

The implication of all this is inescapable. What is genuinely unique has universal significance and must therefore be universally made known, whereas, to quote Visser't Hooft again, "there is no universality if there is no unique event."[13] Thus, uniqueness and universality belong together. It is because Jesus Christ is the only Savior that we are under obligation to proclaim him everywhere. The "inclusivism" of the mission is precisely due to the "exclusivism" of the Mediator. In addition, universal authority over the nations has been given to him; that is why he commissions us to go and make disciples of all the nations (Mt 28:18-20).

Our task is more than to proclaim Christ, however; it is to persuade men (2 Cor 4:5; 5:11). Cormac Murphy-O'Connor, the Roman Catholic Bishop of Arundel and Brighton, has recently written a book on ecumenism in which he quotes a farewell letter from a Greek Catholic bishop in Galilee: "As a Bishop, a preacher of the Gospel, I never tried to convert a Jew or Arab Muslim to Christianity; rather to convert them to be a better Jew, a better Muslim."[14] That is a fantastic misreading of the New Testament. If the apostles (who were of course all Jews) had followed that line, there would never have been a Christian church. Instead, they preached, persuaded and pleaded. So must we. It is impossible for us to be neutral. We are both committed to Christ ourselves and committed to be his advocates, his ambassadors, appealing to people to be reconciled to God (2 Cor 5:20).

## What Evangelism Does Not Mean

Yet this call to the worldwide persuasive preaching of the gospel needs to be hedged round with safeguards. For Christian evangelism has often been abused and in consequence has fallen into disrepute. So let me list six things which the universal proclamation of the unique Christ does *not* mean.

First, it does not mean confusing Christ with culture. Some Western missionaries have made the mistake of exporting with the gospel their whole Western way of life or have (often quite unconsciously) covered their gospel with a cultural overlay. Then their message has been rejected not because it was judged to be false, but because it was perceived to be alien. One does not have to be a crosscultural messenger of the gospel to make the same mistake. We are all creatures of culture and seldom realize how much our outlook and therefore our teaching are conditioned by the background of our race, nationality and class. If our evangelism is to be authentic, we will seek to ensure that our gospel is biblical, not cultural.

Second, true evangelism does not mean that we are imbued with a crusading spirit. Evangelists must not be imperialists, dismissive of other people's cultures, and evangelism should never be either haughty in attitude or aggressive in style. Humility is the preeminent Christian virtue and should characterize all our words and deeds. It is not appropriate to proclaim Christ unless we are manifesting in our proclamation something of his "meekness and gentleness" (2 Cor 10:1). Besides, there is no need to resort to legal or psychological pressure. Truth is sure to prevail in the end. Those who use force of any kind are thereby admitting the weakness of their case.

Third, evangelism does not mean that we do nothing but talk. It is certainly essential to verbalize the gospel, and, since God has himself chosen to speak, Christians should not share the widespread disenchantment with words. Nevertheless, God's Word also became flesh so that his glory was seen. Just so, we cannot announce the good news of God's love if we do not also exhibit it in concrete actions of love. This is a major rationale for combining social action with evangelism. When our light truly shines before men, Jesus said, it is our "good deeds" that they will see and so give glory to our heavenly Father (Mt 5:16).

Fourth, evangelism does not mean that dialogue is excluded. At its simplest, dialogue is a two-way conversation, an exchange between people who are willing to listen as well as speak, to learn as well as teach. Christopher Wright has rightly argued, however, that the "learning" by Christians from non-Christians does not presuppose some "deficiency in the Christian faith as such" so that other religions can add to the biblical revelation. No, "it is one thing to accept that we are fallible and imperfect Christians who need rebuke and challenge, and to be willing to accept it from any quarter. It is quite another to envisage that in dialogue the revelation of God in Christ and the Scriptures needs correction, improvement or addition. It is one thing to challenge *my* faith; another to challenge *the* faith."[15] Readiness to take part in dialogue is a sign of respect for the concerns and convictions of others. Dialogue must neither replace witness nor even rival it as an equal. It is an activity in its own right, whose goal and reward are greater understanding of the other. For the Christian it is also a necessary prelude to witness, for witness becomes wiser and more sensitive as a result.

Fifth, to engage in Christian evangelism does not mean that outside the church we consider God inactive and truth absent. Not at all. God sustains all his creatures, and therefore "is not far from each one of us." By creation "we are his offspring," who "live and move and have our being" in him (Acts 17:27-28). Also Jesus Christ as the Logos of God and the Light of humanity is himself ceaselessly active in the world. Because he is "the true light that gives light to every man" (Jn 1:9), we dare to claim that all beauty, truth and goodness, wherever they are found among human beings, derive from him. This is an aspect of God's "common grace," his love shown to all humankind; it is not, however, "saving grace," which is given only to those who humbly cry to him for mercy.

Sixth, the practice of evangelism does not mean (or at least does not necessarily mean) that we think there is no hope of salvation for those who have never heard of Jesus. What is their position? We can begin by making two points with assurance. First, there is no such thing as self-salvation. All human beings have sinned against the truth they have known, are therefore guilty before God and are "perishing" (that is the argument of Rom 1—3). Nobody can achieve salvation by their own religious observances, good works or sincerity. Those who claim to be Christians on that basis cannot, nor can anyone else. And Cornelius the centurion was not an exception to this rule. His story teaches that salvation is available to Gentiles as well as to

Jews and on the same terms; it does not teach that he attained it by his own righteousness, worship of God, prayers or generosity. On the contrary, he needed to hear the gospel and respond to it in order to receive salvation, life and cleansing (Acts 11:14, 18; 15:9). So self-salvation is impossible.

The second certainty is that Jesus Christ is the only Savior and that salvation is by God's grace alone, on the ground of Christ's cross alone and by faith alone. The only question, therefore, is how much knowledge and understanding of the gospel people need before they can cry to God for mercy and be saved. In the Old Testament people were "justified by faith" even though they had little knowledge or expectation of Christ. Perhaps there are others today in a similar position, who know that they are guilty before God and that they cannot do anything to win his favor, but who in self-despair call upon the God they dimly perceive to save them. If God does save such, as many evangelical Christians believe, their salvation is still only by grace, only through Christ, only by faith. But of course it is hard for people to call on one they have not believed in, or to believe in one of whom they have not heard, or to hear if no one preaches to them (Rom 10:14). It is much easier for people to believe once they have heard the gospel of Christ crucified. It is when they learn from the cross about God's mercy to sinners that they cry "God be merciful to *me,* a sinner!" As Paul put it, "faith comes from hearing the message, and the message is heard through the word of Christ" (Rom 10:17).

These six caveats are necessary to safeguard evangelism from misunderstanding and abuse. But they do not make it one iota less necessary or less urgent. On the contrary, the whole church is committed to take the whole gospel to the whole world. Because of the uniqueness of Jesus Christ, he must be universally made known.

## For Further Reading

Stephen Neill, *Christian Faith and Other Faiths* (IVP, 1984).
Lesslie Newbigin, *The Finality of Jesus Christ* (John Knox, 1969).
W. A. Visser't Hooft, *No Other Name* (Westminster, 1963).

# 7
# CONCLUSION

*I* have almost finished what I have felt impelled to write. Some readers may consider that I have been unnecessarily controversial. For nowadays all kinds of controversy are distasteful and none more so than religious controversy. Yet to shrink from it is characteristic of the age of uncertainty in which we are living, not of Jesus Christ and his apostles; they contended vigorously for what they believed to be the truth. It is not conducive to the health of the church to sweep our differences under the carpet or to pretend that all is sweetness and light when it is not. Nor are these subterfuges consistent with Christian integrity. It is more healthy and more honest to bring our disagreements out into the open. This necessitates being outspoken, without ever needing to be rude. I hope that

in this book I have been consistent with my own principles.

## The Apostles' Authority

Finally, two issues of major importance are at stake.

The first concerns *the authority of Christ's apostles*. That
is why my second chapter is entitled "The First Witnesses." There was a time when all churches recognized
the unique ministry and authority of the apostles as eyewitnesses of the historic Jesus and scribes of the New
Testament. As recently as 1958 the Anglican bishops at
their Lambeth Conference acknowledged that "the
Church is not 'over' the Holy Scriptures, but 'under' them,
in the sense that the process of canonization was not one
whereby the Church conferred authority on the books but
one whereby the Church acknowledged them to possess
authority. And why? The books were recognized as giving the witness of the Apostles to the life, teaching, death,
and resurrection of the Lord and the interpretation by the
Apostles of these events. To that apostolic authority the
Church must ever bow."[1]

Today, however, one often looks in vain for a comparable recognition. To debate what the apostles meant in
their writings, with a view to clarifying it and so to believing and obeying it, is of course essential. But to take the
liberty, having discovered the apostles' teaching, to con-
tradict it is a very different matter. It is the first step on
the slippery slope of pure subjectivism, where there are
no criteria by which to judge what is true and everybody's
opinions seem equally viable. Such a cavalier attitude to
Christ and his apostles, however, is a dangerous modern

innovation. It has always been a characteristic of heretics, but not of church leaders. Until recently, church leaders had a much greater respect for Scripture as "God's Word written" and for tradition as the church's conscientious exposition and application of that Word. To be sure, those issues on which Scripture (and therefore tradition) does not pronounce plainly may rightly be regarded as secondary and as not obligatory for faith, but the articles of the Apostles' Creed (which is a minimal statement of Christian belief confessed by candidates for baptism) do not belong to this category.

Should we not recognize, however, that twentieth-century Christians have different viewpoints, and should we not welcome a comprehensive church which embraces them all? Here we need to distinguish between two different kinds of comprehensiveness. There is a "principled" kind which determines to keep open what Scripture has left open. It becomes "unprincipled," however, when it insists on leaving open what Scripture by its plain teaching has closed. J. I. Packer describes the former as "the *virtue* of tolerating different views on secondary issues on the basis of clear agreement on essentials" and the latter as "the *vice* of retreating from the light of Scripture into an intellectual murk where no outlines are clear, all cats are grey, and syncretism is the prescribed task."[2]

## Christ's Glory

The second serious issue concerns *the glory of Christ himself*. Chapters three to six have all related to him—to his divine-human person, his bodily resurrection, his virgin birth and his uniqueness as the Savior of the world. Luther expressed his own Christ-centeredness in the opening words of his commentary on *Galatians* (1531): "the one doctrine which I have supremely at heart is that of faith in Christ, from whom, through whom and unto whom all my theological thinking flows back and forth, day and night." Would that this were equally true of all theologians today! If the church goes wrong on Christ, it goes wrong on everything. To deny that he is God as well as man is to depart from the very foundation of historic Christianity. To deny the uniqueness of Jesus is to undermine the mission of the church. To deny that Jesus' mother was a virgin or that his tomb was empty is not such a fundamental error, especially in those who believe in the incarnation and (in some sense) in the resurrection. Yet these doctrines are clear in Scripture and in Christian tradition and are therefore not optional. Besides, there are many valid grounds for believing them and none for doubting them. It seems logically absurd to accept the greater miracle (the incarnation) and jib at lesser ones like the virgin birth and the bodily resurrection.

Above all, these deviations from the New Testament are derogatory to the glory of Jesus Christ. God seems to me to be saying to the contemporary church "Touch not my Anointed!" Instead of seeking to edit the New Testament witness to Christ, we should feel what Paul called a "godly jealousy" for his glory, and should have an unshakable resolve to give him the honor which is due his name. In order to do this, we shall have to renounce the folly of fabricating "a Jesus other than the Jesus we [the apostles] preached" (2 Cor 11:1-4) and instead hold fast to the authentic Jesus, who is the Jesus of the apostolic witness.

# Notes

## Chapter One: Introduction: The Present Controversy

[1]John Hick, ed., *The Myth of God Incarnate* (Philadelphia: Westminster, 1978), p. 169.

[2]John Hick, *God and the Universe of Faiths* (New York: St. Martin's Press, 1973), p. 176.

[3]David Jenkins, *The Glory of Man* (New York: Scribners, 1967), p. 99.

[4]David Jenkins, *The Contradiction of Christianity* (London: Student Christian Movement Press, 1976), p. 154.

[5]Lesslie Newbigin, *The Other Side of 1984* (World Council of Churches, 1983), pp. 22, 31.

## Chapter Three: Jesus: Man and God

[1]B. B. Warfield, *The Person and Work of Christ* (Phillipsburg, N.J.: Presbyterian and Reformed, 1950), p. 215.

[2]Ibid., p. 217.

[3]Ibid., p. 237.

[4]Ibid., p. 251.

[5]Donald Coggan, *The Prayers of the New Testament* (New York: Harper and Row, 1967), p. 80.

## Chapter Four: The Resurrection of Jesus Christ

[1]G. E. Ladd, *I Believe in the Resurrection of Jesus* (Grand Rapids, Mich.: Eerdmans, 1975), p. 42.

[2]David Jenkins, "Professors, Bishops and the Search for Truth," *The University of Leeds Review* 27 (1984-85), p. 98.

[3]E. D. Hirsch, *Validity in Interpretation* (New Haven, Conn.:

Yale University Press, 1967), p. 1.

[4]This point is well made by William L. Craig in his article, "The Historicity of the Empty Tomb of Jesus," *New Testament Studies* 31 (1985), pp. 39-67.

[5]E. Earle Ellis, *The Gospel of Luke,* New Century Bible Commentary (Grand Rapids, Mich.: Eerdmans, 1966), p. 273.

[6]C. S. Lewis, *Letters of C. S. Lewis,* ed. W. H. Lewis (New York: Harcourt Brace Jovanovich, 1975), p. 307.

## Chapter Five: The Virgin Birth

[1]Jenkins, "Professors, Bishops," p. 97.

[2]The definition of *midrash* as "a mixture of history and nonhistory" is given by R. H. Gundry in his *Matthew: A Commentary on His Literary and Theological Art* (Grand Rapids, Mich.: Eerdmans, 1982). A critique of his position is made by Philip Barton Payne, entitled "Midrash and History in the Gospels, with special reference to R. H. Gundry's *Matthew,*" in *Gospel Perspectives III,* subtitled "Studies in midrash and historiography," ed. R. T. France and David Wenham (JSOT Press, 1983).

[3]John A. T. Robinson, from an essay entitled "Hosea and the Virgin Birth," in *Twelve More New Testament Studies* (SCM, 1984), pp. 3-4.

[4]Origen, *Contra Celsum* 1.32.

[5]Compare 2 Tim 2:8. For the Old Testament expectation that the Messiah would be descended from David see 2 Sam 7:16; Ps 89:3-4; Is 11:1, 10; Jer 23:5-6. For the New Testament fulfillment, in addition to Lk 1; 2:4 and 3:23-31, see Mt 1:1, 2-16, 20 and Acts 2:30.

[6]C. E. B. Cranfield on Romans 1:4 in the *International Critical Commentary on Romans,* vol. 1 (Edinburgh: T. & T. Clark, 1975), p. 59, n. 1.

## Chapter Six: The Uniqueness of Jesus

[1]Some of these facts and figures are taken from *Towards a Theology for Inter-Faith Dialogue,* a report of a group of the Board for Mission and Unity (Church Information Office,

1984), p. 4.

[2]W. A. Visser't Hooft, *No Other Name* (Philadelphia: Westminster, 1963), p. 11.

[3]Stephen Neill, *Christian Faith and Other Faiths* (Downers Grove, Ill.: InterVarsity Press, 1984), p. 99.

[4]Visser't Hooft, *No Other Name,* pp. 112-13.

[5]Ibid., p. 90.

[6]Ibid., pp. 95-96.

[7]Lesslie Newbigin, *The Finality of Christ* (Richmond, Va.: John Knox, 1969), p. 74.

[8]Neill, *Christian Faith,* p. 23.

[9]*Bhagavad Gita,* trans. Juan Mascaro (New York: Penguin, 1962), pp. 61-62.

[10]Quoted in Visser't Hooft, *No Other Name,* pp. 36-37.

[11]Stephen Neill, writing in the *Church of England Newspaper,* 28 May 1976.

[12]Emil Brunner, *The Mediator* (1927; reprint ed., Philadelphia: Westminster, 1947), pp. 291-99.

[13]Visser't Hooft, *No Other Name,* p. 102.

[14]Cormac Murphy-O'Connor, *The Family of the Church* (England: Darton Longman & Todd, 1984), p. 41.

[15]Christopher Wright in *Anvil* 1, no. 3 (1984): 256.

## Chapter Seven: Conclusion

[1]*The Lambeth Conference Report, 1958* (London: S.P.C.K., 1958), pp. 2-5; from the report of the committee on "The Holy Bible, Its Authority and Message."

[2]J. I. Packer, from his essay entitled "Taking Stock in Theology," in *Evangelicals Today,* ed. John C. King (Lutterworth, 1973), p. 17. See also his *A Kind of Noah's Ark? The Anglican Commitment to Comprehensiveness* (Latimer House, Oxford, 1981).